BEHIND THE SCENES BIOGRAPHIES

WHAT YOU NEVER KNEW ABOUT

>>> ——————— <<<

LEBRON
JAMES

by Helen Cox Cannons

CAPSTONE PRESS
a capstone imprint

Published by Spark, an imprint of Capstone
1710 Roe Crest Drive, North Mankato, Minnesota 56003
capstonepub.com

Library of Congress Cataloging-in-Publication Data
Names: Cox Cannons, Helen, 1971- author.
Title: What you never knew about LeBron James / by Helen Cox Cannons.
Description: North Mankato, Minnesota : Capstone Press, 2025.
Series: Behind the scenes biographies | Includes bibliographical references and index.
Audience: Ages 9–11 | Audience: Grades 4–6
Summary: "He's known as King James. He's the NBA's all-time leading scorer. He's known all
over the world. But what don't you know about LeBron James? Unique facts, carefully leveled
text, and bold photos make this book a slam dunk for all readers"— Provided by publisher.
Identifiers: LCCN 2023046988 (print) | LCCN 2023046989 (ebook) | ISBN 9781669072904
(hardcover) | ISBN 9781669073086 (paperback) | ISBN 9781669072942 (pdf) | ISBN
9781669073093 (epub) | ISBN 9781669073109 (kindle edition)
Subjects: LCSH: James, LeBron—Juvenile literature. | Basketball players—United States—
Biography—Juvenile literature. | African American basketball players—Biography—Juvenile
literature. Classification: LCC GV884.J36 C68 2024 (print) | LCC GV884.J36 (ebook) | DDC
796.323092 [B]—dc23/eng/20231026
LC record available at https://lccn.loc.gov/2023046988
LC ebook record available at https://lccn.loc.gov/2023046989

Editorial Credits
Editor: Christianne Jones; Designer: Elijah Blue; Media Researcher: Jo Miller;
Production Specialist: Whitney Schaefer

Image Credits
Alamy: Barry King, 19, Cinematic, 18, PjrStudio, 12, Storms Media Group, 17, UPI, 15; AP
Photo: Kathy Willens, 22, Tony Dejak, File, 27; Getty Images, 4, Mike Coppola, 10, Ronald
Martinez , 11, Slaven Vlasic, 28; Newscom: Melissa Tamez/Icon Sportswire EGV, 7, RICHARD
B. LEVINE, 25; Shutterstock: A 5, 14, Brocreative, 6, dealona, 24 (shoe), Dfree, 21 (Drake),
Ezvereva, 23, GoodStudio, 29, IIIerlok_xolms, design elements (throughout), Kathy Hutchins,
9, Kolonko, 24 (money), KY726871, 8 (hearts), Mark_KA, 26, mhatzapa, 20, Oleksandr
Panasovskyi, 7 (chart), rvlsoft, 13, s_bukley, 21 (Jay Z), stockphoto-graf, 16, Svetography, 8
(bulldog), Tinseltown, cover, 21 (Lamar)

◇ ◇ ◇ ◇ ◇ ◇ ◇ ◇ ◇ ◇ ◇ ◇ ◇ ◇ ◇ ◇ ◇ ◇ ◇

Printed and bound in China. PO 5827

TABLE OF CONTENTS

Words in **bold** are in the glossary.

BOW DOWN
TO THE KING

LeBron James is one of the greatest basketball players in history. He's not royalty, but people call him King James. That nickname started when he was still in high school.

What else is there to know about LeBron? It's time to find out!

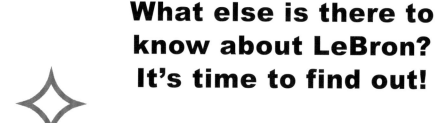

QUIZ TIME

You love LeBron. Prove it!

1. **How tall is LeBron?**

2. **LeBron has had two jersey numbers. What are they?**

3. **What teams has LeBron played for?**

4. **Where did LeBron grow up?**

5. **How many NBA championships has LeBron won?**

1. 6 feet, 9 inches **2.** 23 and 6 **3.** Cleveland Cavaliers, Miami Heat, LA Lakers **4.** Akron, Ohio **5.** four

LEBRON'S LOVES

LeBron married his high school sweetheart, Savannah. They have three children. Sons Bronny and Bryce love basketball. Daughter Zhuri has her own YouTube channel.

FACT
The James family has a French bulldog named Indigo Sky.

Basketball wasn't Lebron's first love. It was football! LeBron was a great football player. The Dallas Cowboys and Seattle Seahawks wanted him to play for them.

MEDIA MASTER

LeBron James ✓
@KingJames

LeBron has a huge following on social media. Check out these numbers!

- Facebook: 27 million

- X (formerly Twitter): 52.6 million

- Instagram: 157 million

But LeBron knows social media can be a distraction. He does not use social media during the NBA playoffs.

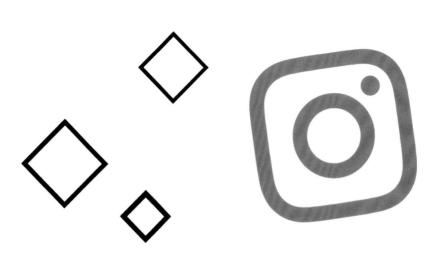

At 17, LeBron was on the cover of *Sports Illustrated* magazine. He was still in high school. The headline was "The Chosen One." He's been on the cover 37 times since then.

BIG MAN **BIKING**

As a kid, LeBron biked all over town. Biking gave him freedom. He still loves biking. LeBron also loves giving back to his community. He leads the Wheels for Education program. It gives bikes and helmets to students in Akron, Ohio. That is his hometown.

SHOOTING STARS AND MUSIC DREAMS

In high school, LeBron played basketball with Dru Joyce III, Willie McGee, Sian Cotton, and Romeo Travis. The group helped their school win its division state basketball championship three times. They called themselves The Fab Five.

FACT

A movie called *Shooting Stars* was made about The Fab Five.

LeBron also loves music. He has a lot of friends in the music business. These friends include Jay-Z, Kendrick Lamar, and Drake. He would love to be a music star himself.

FACT
LeBron listens to classical music or jazz to calm down.

Jay-Z

Kendrick Lamar

Drake

THE BANANA BOAT
CREW

Carmelo Anthony, Dwyane Wade, Chris Paul, and LeBron James are basketball **legends**. They are also good friends. In 2015, the four friends went on vacation. A photo of them riding in a banana boat went **viral**. They are now known as the "Banana Boat Crew."

GETTING DOWN TO
BUSINESS

LeBron isn't just an awesome basketball player. He is also a smart businessman. He's the first active NBA player to be worth more than $1 billion. He has a lifetime deal with Nike. That alone is worth more than $1 billion!

Lots of athletes **promote** products. But LeBron does more than promote when he's involved. He **invests**. He often becomes a partner too. He has a sports nutrition company. He has a TV production company. He even has a pizza company!

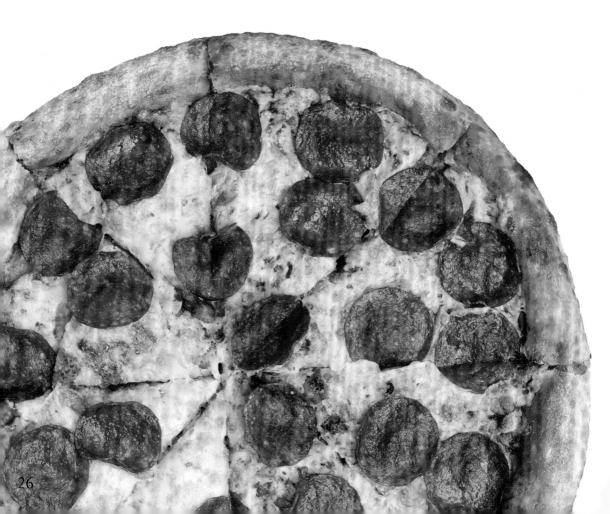

LeBron James and Michelle Obama promoting voting in 2015.

WISE WORDS

"I like criticism. It makes you strong."

"You can't be afraid to fail. It's the only way you succeed—you're not gonna succeed all the time, and I know that."

"All your life they will tell you no. Quite firmly and very quickly. And you will tell them yes."

"People will hate you, rate you, shake you, and break you. But how strong you stand is what makes you."

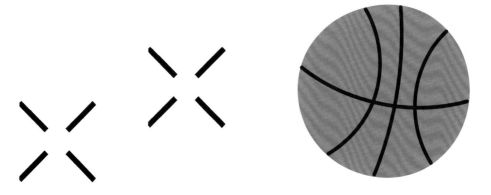

Glossary

invest (in-VEST)—to put money into a business with the hope of getting more money back from it

legend (LEH-juhnd)—someone who is among the best in what they do

promote (pruh-MOHT)—to make people aware of something or someone; promoters are people who plan and raise awareness for events

viral (VYE-ruhl)—quickly and widely spread

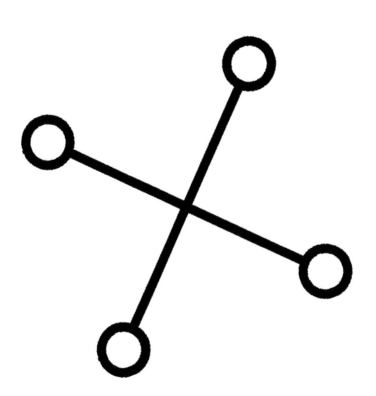

Read More

Fishman, Jon M. *LeBron James*. Minneapolis: Lerner, 2021.

Hubbard, Crystal. *Who Is LeBron James?* New York: Penguin Workshop, 2023.

Steele, Laura Price. *LeBron James*. Mankato, MN: Capstone, 2020.

Internet Sites

Kiddle: LeBron James Facts for Kids
kids.kiddle.co/LeBron_James

The LeBron James Family Foundation
lebronjamesfamilyfoundation.org

LeBron James Official Site
lebronjames.com

Index

About the Author

Helen Cox Cannons was born in Dumfriesshire, Scotland. She has a Master's Degree in English Literature from the University of Edinburgh. She has worked as an editor and author for more than 25 years. Helen likes to crochet, sing, go for country walks, and fuss over her two cats, Nero and Diego, and trusty hound, Alba. She now lives in Oxfordshire with her two daughters, Abby and Serena.